God's

Covenant

With His People

God's

Covenant

With

His

People

Walking in Covenant Relationship with God

Written by

Dr. Annette Skinner-Coleman

Copyright

Printed in the United States of America

First Printing, 2016

ISBN-13: 978-1-942022-26-8

ISBN10: 1942022263

the **Butterfly** Typeface

The Butterfly Typeface Publishing
PO BOX 56193
Little Rock Arkansas 72215

Dedication

To my mother Enid Evans Cave Skinner, a woman who believed in her God to guide her in all her ways. She displayed a love and trust for Jesus Christ that left a lasting legacy and impression on all who came in contact with her. My love for Jesus Christ was planted by the seeds that Ma-ma sowed in my life.

I also dedicate this book to all of my future grandchildren that they may know and walk in a loving relationship with Jesus Christ.

Use the Sword of the Spirit

(the Word of the Lord)

to unlock the treasures

of the Kingdom

But we have this treasure in earthen vessels, that the excellency of the power may be of God and not of us.

2 Corinthians 4:7

King James Version (KJV)

Table of Contents

Foreword

The covenant of God is an unlocking and releasing of kingdom principles to the body of Christ. God did not leave His people without a hope and a future.

This book releases spiritual truths reminding us of our covenant relationship with our Heavenly Father. It also reminds us of the benefits and blessings between God and His covenant people. It does not matter how dark the world may become before the return of Christ, God's covenant people has His promise that their covenant with God will never fail. The message in this book will unlock the revelation of covenant principles and the power of God who is a covenant relationship with His children.

My desire as a Pastor and Prophetic Teacher is to reconnect the Body of Christ to Jesus who is the head of the body of His church. As I read "God's Covenant with His people", I realized that this was not just another Christian book teaching on the covenant of God, but a life giving organism being imparted to us by the Spirit of God. It is a message given to His servant, whom He could trust to write with accuracy and simplicity of the Gospel.

This message will speak to the new converts giving them clarity of God's Covenant whom He delivered to all humanity. The message infiltrates the mind of theology and replace it with the Word and work of God that will continue until Jesus returns.

This message is from God and should be added to every Bible study and book store shelf. All humanity should know of God's great love for the world and turn to Jesus because the Covenant of God is still active. This message is a blessing, revealing God's love and benefits for His covenant people.

Dr. Dorothy Batts
Pastor, Outreach for Jesus Church
and Christian Education Center, Inc.
Hope Mills, North Carolina

Foreword

The revelation of understanding covenant relationship is expressed and explained in this book. This covenant relationship is one that carries eternal benefits with someone who is always faithful. The author expresses revelation knowledge that all believers need for continual spiritual growth and development in a divine covenant relationship. I encourage all who read this book to pass it on to encourage others seeking a true divine covenant.

Pastor Aileen Lyons
Everlasting Life Gospel Ministries
Fayetteville, North Carolina

Acknowledgments

As I reflect on God's goodness to me, I must acknowledge the love and support of my biological and church family. My loving husband Ron, beautiful and Godly daughter Zoë, my sisters Marva, Lena, Ju-Ann, niece Lisa, cousin Shirley and adopted sister Lilly. Thank you Pastor Batts and all my church family at Outreach for Jesus Church and Christian Education Center, Inc.

Introduction

O ur God is a God of covenant and relationship. In the beginning God created the heavens and the earth:

Then God said, Let us make man in our image, according to our likeness, let them have dominion over the fish of the sea, over the birds of the air, and over every creeping thing that creeps on the earth.

Genesis 1:26

Here we see the beginning of covenant relationship between God and man. God created man and placed them in the garden, there God gave them authority and a charge.

And God blessed them, and God said unto them, Be fruitful, and multiply, and replenish the earth, and subdue it: and have dominion over the fish of the sea, and over the fowl of the air, and over every living thing that moveth upon the earth.

Genesis 1:28

We are aware and have studied how Adam and Eve fell in the Garden. That did not stop the covenant relationship established by God with man, who He created in his own image.

The first time the word covenant is mentioned in the Old Testament is when God was speaking with Noah:

*But with thee will I establish my **covenant**; and thou shalt come into the ark, thou, and thy sons, and thy wife, and thy sons' wives with thee.*

Genesis 6:18

The Covenant did not start with Abraham being called out of the Ur by God. As a matter of fact, Abraham and his father were on their way to Canaan when his father settled in Haran:

Terah took his son Abram, his grandson Lot son of Haran, and his daughter-in-law Sarai, the wife of his son Abram, and together they set out from Ur of the Chaldeans to go to Canaan. But when they came to Haran, they settled there.

Genesis 11:30-32

Ask yourself, "Where have you settled on the way or path that God has ordained for your destiny, purpose and the plan of God's covenant?"

He also said to him, "I am the Lord, who brought you out of Ur of the Chaldeans to give you this land to take possession of it.

Genesis 15:6-8

God told Abram why He brought him out. Although Abram and his seed will be blessed, the ultimate purpose was God's will in the establishment and fulfilling of His plan. From this Abram and his seed will be blessed,

*In the same day the LORD made a **covenant** with Abram, saying, Unto thy seed have I given this land, from*

the river of Egypt unto the great river, the river Euphrates:

Genesis 15:18

*And I will make my **covenant** between me and thee, and will multiply thee exceedingly.*

Genesis 17:2

Abram had to walk in faith, his faith and belief in God was counted to him as righteousness. We need both faith and righteousness to walk in obedience. Like Abram who was later called Abraham, let us chose to believe and follow God.

Many of us believe, but stop short in our journey, purpose and progress. Just like with Abraham the lapse of time does not halt or hinder God's covenant. The only thing that can hinder our possession of what God has for us is our obedience to Him.

Now even if you realized that you have stopped or settled short at your Haran, believe God and move on in faith.

A Covenant

What is a covenant? A covenant is a promise that is sanctioned by an oath. A dictionary can only give the definition of a covenant based on man's understanding. However, we need a revelation of God's covenant (His binding word) to us. God's covenant is divine ordinance with signs or pledges covenant.

Knowing that there is a covenant is not enough. Knowing the words and your entitlements of the covenant are important. It is crucial, we must know and walk in the entitlement of the covenant.

However, we must have faith that the God of the promised covenant will fulfill His word. He is His word, and since it is impossible for God to lie, it is impossible for the covenant to fail - on God's part!

In the same way God, desiring even more to show the heirs of the promise the unchangeableness of His purpose, interposed with an oath, so that by two unchangeable things in which it is impossible for God to lie, we who have taken refuge would have strong encouragement to take hold of the hope set before us.

Hebrews 6:18-19

Faith is needed to walk in the covenant and it comes from hearing the Word of God. It is ok to know that there is a will, as outlined in the Old and New Testaments, but you must read, study and meditate on it day and night. This is how you pave the way to make yourself prosper - the Word makes it happen!

The Word of God will prosper in the thing that God has sent it to do. When the enemy comes to question or try to cause you to question your covenant entitlements, allow the Holy Spirit to adjudicate and probate your entitlements.

Adjudicate is a legal term that means to make official decisions of your rights, whereas probate is a judicial determination which validates the will (covenant).

God encouraged, admonished and commanded Joshua:

There shall not any man be able to stand before thee all days of thy life: as I was with Moses, so I will be with thee: I will not fail thee, nor forsake thee.

Be strong and of a good courage: for unto this people shalt thou divide for an inheritance the land, which I swear unto their fathers to give them.

Only be thou strong and very courageous, that thou mayest observe to do according to all the law, which Moses my servant commanded thee: turn not from it to the right hand or to the left, that thou mayest prosper withersoever thou goest.

This book of the law shall not depart out of thy mouth; but thou shalt meditate therin day and night, that thou mayest observe to do according to all that is written therin: for then thou shalt make thy way prosperous, and then thou shalt have good success.

Have not I commanded thee? Be strong and of a good courage; be not afraid, neither be thou dismayed: for the LORD thy God is with thee withersoever thou goest.

Joshua 1:5-9

Joshua knew that just because Moses died that the Covenant and promises of God did not go away. Joshua had a purpose and task as planned by God that led to the fulfillment of a covenant promise. As with Joshua God has a purpose for us, it is tied to His Covenant with His people. At this time, Joshua was encouraged and directed by God 1) be **strong** and 2) be of good **courage**.

You must know why Joshua was encouraged. It was because the God who called him and appointed him for the covenant purpose, promised never to leave him. The same promise is to you today.

When Jesus gave the great commission to His disciples, He said, *"Lo I am with you even until the end of the world."*

Matthew 28:20

Who is 'I Am that I Am?'

'I Am that I Am' is the God that is present to be whatever He needs to give to you in that present time in fulfillment of His covenant promise and purpose.

'I Am that I Am' is your creator **(Genesis 1:1; Isaiah 54:5)** and your redeemer, *I the Lord am thy Savior and thy Redeemer:* **Isaiah 49:26**

'I Am that I Am' is your guide: *Make me know your ways, O Lord; Teach me your paths. Lead me in Your truth and team me, for you are the God of my salvation; For you I wait all the day.* **Psalms 25:4-5**

'I Am that I Am' is your Strength: *The LORD is my strength and my shield; My heart trusts in Him, and I am helped; Therefore, my heart exults, And with my song I shall thank Him.*

'I Am that I Am' *is* Your protector and your deliverer: *God is our refuge and strength a very present help in trouble.*

Psalms 46:1

'I Am that I Am' will not fail you: *Be strong and courageous, do not be afraid or tremble at them, for the LORD your God is the one who goes with you He will not fail you or forsake you.*

Deuteronomy 31:6

'I Am that I Am' *is* Your peace and your hope:

Truly my soul finds rest in God;

My salvation comes from him.

Truly he is my rock and my salvation;

He is my fortress; I will never be shaken.

Psalms 62: 1- 2; 5-6

Since the God of Covenant, the only True and Living God, is all this and more, how can we not walk in what He has prepared for us?

Things to think about:

- Are you in a covenant with God?
- What does this covenant mean to you?
- Do you have faith in God's word, to believe that you are entitled to every area of the covenant, because of what Christ did for you on the cross?

Jesus' blood was shed for you (a new covenant)

And when He had taken a cup and given thanks, He gave it to them, and they drank from it. And He said to them, "This is My blood of the covenant, which is poured out for many."

Mark 14:23-24

Notes:

_____

_____

_____

_____

_____

_____

_____

The Holy Spirit

What is the Holy Spirit revealing? Holy Spirit is here to guide us in the truths of the covenant. My husband and I are parents. As parents who walk in obedience to God, we cannot take our child to her destiny but we can start the process by leading her in the direction that God wants her to go.

Parents, we must let our children know about the covenant relationship with Jesus Christ and God's purpose for their life. We are required to raise them in an atmosphere that honors God and His Word. We should walk in obedience, faith, love and especially give glory to God. So many honor their gifts above God who is the gift giver and sustainer of their gifts.

As Abraham's descendants went on to possess the land of the covenant so shall our seed walk in and possess the covenant promises of God even if we may not see the full manifestation in our lifetime.

At the time God called Abraham out, it was just the fullness of time for the initiation of the covenant that would continue between God and the natural and spiritual Israel.

God had a covenant with Abraham. Abraham was called the friend of God not because of the covenant, but because of his obedience to the Covenant Maker. Obedience is the highest form of worship.

Even though Abraham had a covenant, the spiritual element of faith had to be present. Abraham believed God and it was accounted to him unto righteousness. God will give us what we need, but we must acknowledge and honor Him in all of our ways.

Notice how God Himself instructed Abraham on even how to worship Him. The Holy Spirit is our guide, teacher and Paraclete who will lead us into all truths. What are these truths? Jesus said, *"I am the way, the truth and the life."* Here we see again **'I AM'.**

And if I go and prepare a place for you, I will come again, and receive you unto myself; that where I am, there ye may be also.

And whither I go ye know, and the way ye know.

Thomas saith unto him, Lord, we know not whither thou goest; and how can we know the way?

Jesus saith unto him, **I am** *the way, the truth, and the life: no man cometh unto the Father, but by me.*

John 14:3-6

The Truths

What is your part concerning the truth?

The truths are in **THE TRUTH** (Christ Himself), the *WWW* (*Will, Worship, Walk*) of it all.

The Holy Spirit reveals the Will of the Father, teaches us how to worship the Father and how to walk in obedience to the Will of the Father.

In light of your relationship with Christ, take a real look at your *WWW* (*Will, Worship, and Walk*).

Is your will, the will of the Covenant keeping God?

Does your worship reflect that He alone is your God or are you trying to have covenant with another god (idol)?

Another god can be yourself, your talent, your gifts, your looks, your wealth. I can go on and on, in other words another god "idol" is anything or one that you give more reverence and honor to than I Am that I am, the Lord God Almighty!

If your *will* and your *worship* is God and Christ centered, your *walk* will be that of a person who wants to be obedient to the covenant relationship with the Father. You can achieve this only by the power of the Holy Spirit.

Things to think about:

- Who is the Holy Spirit?
- The Holy Spirit is God, the third Person of the Trinity. As God, the Holy Spirit can truly function as the Comforter and Counselor that Jesus promised He would be (John 14:16, 26, 15:26).
- What was God's covenant with Abraham?
- What are the 'truths'?
- Have you ever asked God how He wants to fulfill His covenant with and throughout you?
- What truths of your WWW (Will, Worship and Walk) are you unclear, uncertain or unsure of? Ask God for a revelation of these things.

Notes:

_____

_____

_____

_____

_____

_____

_____

_____

Walking in the Covenant

The Holy Spirit is saying that all of the Word of God is His Covenant. The Holy Spirit lets us know that if we focus just on the Abrahamic Covenant we are focusing on just one aspect of the covenant.

Neither can we focus just on the Davidic Covenant the natural covenant that God made with David in **2 Samuel 7: 12-17**. Did not Christ come to fulfill the law? Everything is fulfilled in Christ.

Do not think that I have come to abolish the Law or the prophets; I have not come to abolish them but to fulfill them.

Matthew 5:17

Let us look at these words and the work of the person of Christ for us:

Redemption

This is the exchange act of Christ that saves us Christ hath redeemed us from the curse of the law, being made a curse for us: for it is written,

Cursed is every one that continueth not in all things which are written in the book of law to do them: That the blessing of Abraham might come on the Gentiles through Jesus Christ; that we might receive the promise of the Spirit through faith.

Galatians 3:10, 14

Reconciliation

To restore friendship, harmony, to make consistent and congruent.

For it was the Father's good pleasure for all the fullness to dwell in Him, and through Him to reconcile and all things to Himself, having made peace through the blood of His cross; through Him, I say, whether things on earth or things in heaven. And although you were formerly alienated and hostile in mind, engaged in evil deeds.

Colossians 1:19-21

Position

A situation that confers rank or status, the act of placing in a relative place, situation or standing, official rank or status. Our position is in Christ.

Look at what Christ did for us!

God, who is rich in mercy, for his great love wherewith he loved us, Even when we were dead in sins, hath quickened us together with Christ, (by grace ye are saved;) And hath raised us up together, and made us sit together in heavenly places in Christ Jesus:

Ephesians 2:4-6

But you have your very being in Him:

For in him we live and move, and have our being; as certain also of your own poets have said, For we are also his offspring. Forasmuch then as we are the offspring of God, we ought not to think that the Godhead is like unto gold, or silver, or stone graven by art and man's device.

Acts 17:28-29

Christ redeemed us by His blood, reconciled us back to the right relationship with the Father and then positioned us in Him in Heavenly places.

It is from this position that we have Covenant relationship with the Father, for we are seated in heavenly places in Christ Jesus.

This is a position of covenant relationship as sons of God, Christ being our High Priest and mediator of the New Covenant.

Relationship with the Father leads to revelation and this revelation shows us how to walk in the manifestation of what I call "Covenant Rights".

Let's Look At An Example

Let us take another look at Joshua. One of the covenant rights he had to walk in was "**be strong**". Joshua did not have the written word like we do today. All he had to go on was God's covenant promise. He believed God and went forward to fulfill his own task for God's purpose.

Joshua was **strong** in faith believing God to be with him as he led a nation of chosen people into their land of inheritance. This inheritance was spoken of by Abraham over 430 hundred years before the beginning of the exodus from Egypt.

Yet as you read, sadly the tribes went into the land of promise but never *fully possessed* the land of covenant.

Don't allow the enemies of doubt, discouragement, disobedience, lack of worship or lack of knowledge of the Word of God cause you to not possess your promised possessions.

Things to think about:

- What role does Christ play in the covenant?
- Do you realize that He is the mediator of the New Covenant?
- How does the Holy Spirit relate to the covenant?
- Review Acts chapter 1 and Acts Chapter 2.
- Does the Holy Spirit give us power to be witnesses to the New Covenant?
- What is our position with Christ within the covenant?

Notes:

_____

_____

_____

_____

_____

_____

_____

_____

The Covenant of God
The Dominion of Man

In the beginning God gave dominion to man. Please read **Genesis 1**. The Adamic fall came into place when Eve was deceived and Adam disobeyed. However, Christ came as the second Adam that we could walk in newness of life and fellowship with the father.

And so it is written, the first man Adam was made a living soul; the last Adam was made a quickening spirit.

1 Corinthians 15:44-46

Christ has reconciled us back to the Father.

What does this have to do with the Covenant?

Well, God is the covenant keeping God and if we now have power to become the sons of God, we have the right as sons and the authority to walk in the power of Christ, having dominion and exercising authority.

He was in the world, and the world was made by him, and the world knew him not.

He came unto his own, and his own received him not.

But as many as received Him, to them gave He power to become the sons of God, even to them that believe on his name:

John 1:10

You not only have power to be a son but you have been given power over the enemy.

Behold, I give unto you power to tread on serpents and scorpions, and over all the power of the enemy: and nothing shall by any means hurt you.

Luke 10:19

Authority and dominion comes through obedience to the Word of God.

You must acknowledge and walk in the authority by faith. "Sonship" does have its privileges, especially for those who walk in the will of the Father.

Going back to Genesis, covenant started with God's words, *"Let us create man in OUR image"*. However, misused power and authority does not lead to possessing the covenant. Redemption came and reconciliation was made with God and man through Jesus Christ.

What is the purpose of reconciliation? Is it just to acknowledge that we are at peace with God?

No, reconciliation brings you to the position of peace with God, to walk in the authority He has given us as His chosen covenant children.

God's covenant does not go away, however, if we are not in right relationship with Christ, walking in and by faith, the covenant promises may seem fleeting.

Remember this:

Covenant is *initiated* by God.

Covenant is *maintained* by God's word, He said I AM the Lord I change not.

Covenant is *fulfilled* by God's word.

Jesus, the Word that became flesh and dwelt among us, stated that He came to fulfill the law.

Things to think about:

- What is dominion? The Hebrew word Qal means to have dominion, rule, tread down, dominate and subjugate.
- How is Christ the 'second' Adam and how does that affect you?
- Read 1 Corinthians Chapter 15. Meditate on these verses from the chapter.

And so it is written, The first man Adam was made a living soul; the last Adam was made a quickening spirit. Howbeit that was not first which is spiritual, but that which is natural; and afterward that which is spiritual. The first man is of the earth, earthy; the second man is the Lord from heaven.

- What power do we have as sons of Christ? Read John chapter 1.

Notes:

_____

_____

_____

_____

_____

_____

_____

Christ,
The Anointed One

There is not one specific scripture that points out all that the covenant encompasses, but there is one act that entitles us to walk in the covenant:

The death, burial and resurrection of Christ the Anointed One

That event (not three separate acts) was planned by the Father to redeem man to Himself in Christ before the foundation of the world.

And you, that were sometime alienated and enemies in your mind by wicked works, yet now hath he reconciled

Colossians 1:21

For the law of the Spirit of life in Christ Jesus hath made me free from the law of sin and death. For what the law could not do, in that it was weak through the flesh, God sending his own Son in the likeness of sinful flesh, and for sin, condemned sin in the flesh: That the righteousness of the law might be fulfilled in us, who walk not after the flesh, but after the Spirit. For they that are after the flesh do mind the things of the flesh; but they that are after the Spirit the things of the Spirit. For to be carnally minded is death; but to be spiritually minded is life and peace. Because the carnal mind is enmity against God: for it is not subject to the law of God, neither indeed can be. So then they that are in the flesh cannot please God.

Romans 8

God's enemies (enemies of the Word, anti-Christ) have no place in the covenant relationship. We WERE enemies in our mind because of our actions- carnal not subject to God. Imagine sons who are entitled to a covenant relationship but in their ignorance of these entitlements they are walking in opposition and taking a war stance against the Heavenly Father.

And all things are of God, who hath reconciled us to himself by Jesus Christ, and hath given to us the ministry of reconciliation.

2 Corinthians 5:18

For if, when we were enemies, we were reconciled to God by the death of his Son, much more, being reconciled, we shall be saved by his life.

Romans 5:10

In essence if you are not in right relationship with Christ you have positioned yourself (in your mind) to oppose all that you can have. However, according to **Isaiah 10: 27**, The anointing of God destroys the yolk. So Christ is the anointed one who destroys the yolks in our life.

Christ is the mediator of the new covenant **(Hebrew 12:24)**, allow Him to destroy every yolk. Give Him your burdens and accept your position in Him and the covenant relationship as a son of God.

*And to Jesus the
mediator of the new
covenant, and to the
blood of sprinkling,
that speaketh better
things than that
of Abel*

Things to think about:

- Do you believe you are redeemed?
- What does the covenant encompass?
- What does it mean to be 'reconciled'?
- This is a fact you were reconciled for a purpose – the purpose of God!

Notes:

_____

_____

_____

_____

_____

_____

_____

_____

Abide in the Word

The Holy Spirit is encouraging you to abide, Jesus told us to abide in Him. Study and meditate upon the word of God (know the terms of God's covenant with you).

Unless you abide, you cannot produce fruit and manifest the Word of God. Abiding in the word is not quoting scriptures, it is living in relationship and revelation. Relationship with the Father and revelation of His will for your life.

No one can pour or teach it into you, the Holy Spirit reveals the will of the Father to you.

As a beginning point pray **(Psalms 119:33-35 *and* verses 17-18)**, study and ask God to give you revelation of what He has predestinated you to walk in **(John 1:12, John 15, Ephesians 1, Colossians 1 and Luke 10:19)**.

Read and meditate on these scriptures:

Teach me, O Lord, the way of thy statutes; and I shall keep it unto the end. Give me understanding, and I shall keep thy law; yea, I shall observe it with my whole heart. Make me to go in the path of thy commandments; for therin do I delight.

Psalms 119:33-35, 17-18

But as many as received him, to them gave he power to become the sons of God, even to them that believe on his name:

John 1:12

Behold, I give unto you power to tread on serpents and scorpions, and over all the power of the enemy: and nothing shall by any means hurt you.

Luke 10:19

You are redeemed and reconciled so that you can abide in the position of the covenant. Abide in the Word of God. I stated earlier that Jesus is the Truth. The Truth is also the Word that became flesh and dwelt among us. Now the Word is dwelling, living and abiding in us.

Abide in the Word that has abided in you. The person of Christ wants to bring you to the place of abiding in His Covenant which is His Word.

Things to think about:

- How do you abide?
- How do you meditate and study His Word daily?
- By answering these questions, you can bring into focus those areas you need the Holy Spirit to help you.

Notes:

_____

_____

_____

_____

_____

_____

_____

_____

Entitlements

of the

Covenant

D o you know your entitlements of the covenant?

Some of them include:

deliverance, protection, prosperity, healing, wisdom, salvation, and authority over the power of the enemy, the ability to walk in love, lights to the world, and salt to the earth, whole household saved etc.

I may need healing, you may need protection and another may need a financial breakthrough. It is in the covenant.

Again, the Holy Spirit is saying that the Covenant is more than the blessing of Abraham as some sing and say.

It is all in Christ Jesus.

Since **John 1 verse 1** says that He is the Word and that He was with God and is God, get to know the Word!

Get in the right position and relationship with your God.

Here are a few references:

Jeremiah 29:11

Isaiah Chapter 54

John Chapter 15

Romans 8:1-17

Colossians Chapter 1

Ephesians Chapter 1

Conclusion

The study of the covenant cannot be completed on one sheet or within one book; it is in the relationship with the only covenant keeping God, The Lord God Almighty, the only True and Living God and His son Jesus Christ.

Being guided by His Precious Holy Spirit, I encourage you to use the Word of the Lord as the two edged sword and unlock the treasures of heaven which enables you and your seed to walk in your covenant right with God.

As with Abraham, Jacob, David and the Apostles this is a process.

Don't stop in Haran as Abram's father did. Proceed to your area of covenant blessings.

Proceed walking in obedience to the Word that you may produce fruit and your fruit may remain.

God's Kingdom has come. Now let His will be done in your earth.

Remember this:

God = the covenant giver and the covenant keeper.

Abraham = faithful servant and obedient, he is the covenant possessor and friend of God.

Now we have the same promise, enter into it by faith.

(Place your name) = faithful and obedient servant, (place your name) the covenant possessor and friend of God.

Things to think about:

- Has this book been helpful to you?
- Do you know your area of covenant blessings?
- Are you ready to bear fruit?
- Your fruit will bear the image of the One that created you. God said let US create man in our image.

Notes:

Thy Kingdom Come
Thy Will Be Done

A Prayer

Father in the name of Jesus

according to the word of your covenant,

I pray that the Holy Spirit will open

the eyes of my understanding

that I may understand and know

the hope of my calling in Christ Jesus.

Teach me your statues and I will keep them

until the end.

Continue to order my steps in your word

as I study to show myself approved

unto God a workman that is not ashamed

of the Gospel.

I thank you that every promise

in you is yea and Amen.

That you watch over your word to perform it

and your word shall not return unto you

void of fulfilling your purpose in my life.

In Jesus name,

Amen

God remembers His Covenant

Children of God I want you to read and meditate on these truths from the Word of God to add to your faith and confidence in your God:

And God heard their groaning, and God remembered his covenant with Abraham, with Isaac, and with Jacob.

Exodus 2: 24

When thou art in tribulation, and all these things are come upon thee, even in the latter days, if thou turn to the Lord thy God, and shalt be obedient unto his voice; (For the Lord thy God is a merciful God;) he will not forsake thee, neither destroy thee, nor forget the covenant of thy fathers which he sware unto them.

Deuteronomy 4:30-31 KJV

He shall cry unto me, Thou art my father, my God, and the rock of my salvation. My mercy will I keep for him for evermore, and my covenant shall stand fast with him. His seed also will I make to endure for ever, and his throne as the days of heaven. If his children forsake my law, and walk not in my judgments; If they break my statutes, and keep not my commandments; Then will I visit their transgression with the rod, and their iniquity with stripes. Nevertheless, my lovingkindness will I not utterly take from him, nor suffer my faithfulness to fail. My covenant will I not break, nor alter the thing that is gone out of my lips.

Psalms 89:26, 28-34 KJV

Seek the Lord, and his strength: seek his face evermore. Remember his marvellous works that he hath done; his wonders, and the judgments of his mouth; He hath remembered his covenant for ever, the word which he commanded to a thousand generations.

Psalms 105:4-5, 8 KJV

Established by God:

The covenant was established by God.

And so all Israel shall be saved: as it is written, There shall come out of Sion the Deliverer, and shall turn away ungodliness from Jacob: For this is my covenant unto them, when I shall take away their sins.

For who hath known the mind of the Lord? or who hath been his counsellor? Or who hath first given to him, and it shall be recompensed unto him again? For of him, and through him, and to him, are all things: to whom be glory forever. Amen.

Romans 11:26-27, 34-36 KJV

The Covenant in our Hearts

The covenant is no longer carried in an ark, but in our hearts.

Behold, the days come, saith the Lord, that I will make a new covenant with the house of Israel, and with the house of Judah: Not according to the covenant that I made with their fathers in the day that I took them by the hand to bring them out of the land of Egypt; which my covenant they brake, although I was an husband unto them, saith the Lord: But this shall be the covenant that I will make with the house of Israel; After those days, saith the Lord, I will put my law in their inward parts, and write it in their hearts; and will be their God, and they shall be my people.

Jeremiah 31:31-33 KJV

Children of the Covenant

But ye are not in the flesh, but in the Spirit, if so be that the Spirit of God dwell in you. Now if any man have not the Spirit of Christ, he is none of his.

For as many as are led by the Spirit of God, they are the sons of God. For ye have not received the spirit of bondage again to fear; but ye have received the Spirit of adoption, whereby we cry, Abba, Father. The Spirit itself beareth witness with our spirit, that we are the children of God: And if children, then heirs; heirs of God, and joint-heirs with Christ; if so be that we suffer with him, that we may be also glorified together.

Romans 8:9, 14-17 KJV

For ye are all the children of God by faith in Christ Jesus. For as many of you as have been baptized into Christ have put on Christ. There is neither Jew nor Greek, there is neither bond nor free, there is neither male nor female: for ye are all one in Christ Jesus. And if ye be Christ's, then are ye Abraham's seed, and heirs according to the promise.

Galatians 3:26-29 KJV

Now we, brethren, as Isaac was, are the children of promise.

Galatians 4:28 KJV

Old Testament

For those who think the Covenant is just for the Old and New Testament, know that Jesus is the mediator of the New and Living Covenant.

Now of the things which we have spoken this is the sum: We have such a high priest, who is set on the right hand of the throne of the Majesty in the heavens; a minister of the sanctuary, and of the true tabernacle, which the Lord pitched, and not man.

But now hath he obtained a more excellent ministry, by how much also he is the mediator of a better covenant, which was established upon better promises. For if that first covenant had been faultless, then should no place have been sought for the second. For finding fault with them, he saith, Behold, the days come, saith the Lord, when I will make a new covenant with the house of Israel and with the house of Judah: not according to the covenant that I made with their fathers, in the day when I took them by the hand to lead them out of the land of Egypt; because they continued not in my covenant, and I regarded them not, saith the Lord.

For this is the covenant that I will make with the house of Israel after those days, saith the Lord; I will put my laws into their mind, and write them in their hearts: and I will be to them a God, and they shall be to me a people:

Hebrews 8:1-2, 6-10 KJVA

Other Scriptures

For if that first covenant had been faultless, then should no place have been sought for the second.

For finding fault with them, he saith, Behold, the days come, saith the Lord, when I will make a new covenant with the house of Israel and with the house of Judah:

Not according to the covenant that I made with their fathers in the day when I took them by the hand to lead them out of the land of Egypt; because they continued not in my covenant, and I regarded them not, saith the Lord.

For this is the covenant that I will make with the house of Israel after those days, saith the Lord; I will put my laws into their mind, and write them in their hearts: and I will be to them a God, and they shall be to me a people:

Hebrews 8:10

But ye are come unto mount Zion, and unto the city of the living God, the heavenly Jerusalem, and to an innumerable company of angels,

To the general assembly and church of the firstborn, which are written in heaven, and to God the Judge of all, and to the spirits of just men made perfect,

And to Jesus the mediator of the new covenant, and to the blood of sprinkling, that speaketh better things than that of Abel.

Hebrews 12:24

About the Author

D r. Annette Skinner-Coleman is a wife, mother and author. She is also a school counselor and an ordained minister.

Her vision is that through her writing and her life, others see God and not her. She resides in North Carolina.

Visit Dr. Skinner-Coleman's Facebook author page for more author information.

www.facebook.com/ascolemanbooks

ζωή

Judge Zoe

Contact

Butterfly Typeface Publishing

for all your

publishing & writing needs!

Iris M Williams

PO Box 56193

Little Rock AR 72215

www.butterflytypeface.com

the Butterfly Typeface